S

G16/97

Published by
The Royal Yachting Association
RYA House Ensign way Hamble
Southampton SO31 4YA
Tel: 0845 345 0400 Fax: 0845 345 0329
Email: info@rya.org.uk Web: www.rya.org.uk
© 1990 Royal Yachting Association

The RYA National Powerboat Scheme was updated in January 1996, replacing the previous RYA Sportsboat Scheme. This booklet replaces the previous edition (G16/83).

Throughout this book the pronouns 'he', 'him' and 'his' have been used inclusively and are intended to apply to both men and women. It is important in sport as elsewhere that women and men should have equal status and equal opportunities.

Text and cover photo by John Driscoll
Illustrations by Maxine Kilburn
Photographs by Tony Dallimore

CONTENTS

"It was a hot summer afternoon. The crew of the club rescue boat, keen to get a cool drink, decided that nothing was going to happen to the remaining competitors in the race. After all, even if someone did capsize, they would probably welcome the chance to cool off in the lake.

"As the rescue boat crew walked into the clubhouse, an over-enthusiastic roll tack by one of the tailenders dunked helmsman and crew in the water, with the boat quickly inverting on top of them.

"The helmsman, nose broken by the boom and dazed, still managed to duck under the hull and surface clear; his crew, trapped face down in a tangle of rope and wire, did not. By the time the rescue boat crew reached the dinghy, it was too late."

No, it hasn't happened, but this book is intended to help prevent fiction like that from ever becoming fact.

Safety boats form an integral part of dinghy sailing and windsurfing activities, from the instruction of novices at sailing centres to club racing and championships.

Those operating such boats clearly take on a responsibility towards others, yet they must not forget their responsibility towards themselves. Crews have been killed or injured when providing safety cover for others who remained unharmed.

As part of its wide range of training schemes, the RYA offers a course for safety and rescue boat crews within the National Powerboat Scheme.

The Safety Boat Course is intended for amateur crews providing safety cover for club activities and sailing instructors working with groups of inexperienced sailors and windsurfers. It should give you the skills to carry out individual rescues, fleet safety cover and race management duties.

The aim of this handbook is to provide advice to anyone involved in providing a safety boat back-up for dinghy sailing and windsurfing. Although it details all the techniques covered in the Safety Boat Course it should be used in conjunction with those courses, rather than instead of them. No publication is a realistic substitute for practical instruction and experience.

The book has been divided into three parts. Part One - Strategy, deals with all the long term issues which affect safety boat operations. Part Two - Tactics covers the practical techniques needed on the water while Part Three - References is a source of additional information relevant to both previous sections.

Throughout the book, a distinction is made between rescue and safety. The former implies urgent, possibly immediate, action where there is risk to life. The latter implies support to prevent or minimise injury or damage. In practical terms, the vast majority of clubs and schools provide support boats, which spend most of their time on safety duties, but are occasionally used for rescues.

The full range of equipment suggested in this book and the most extreme techniques needed for coastal support work may not be appropriate to the inland club coxswain working in a very restricted area.

That is the main reason why the RYA does not issue a standard set of "safety guidelines" for sailing and windsurfing clubs or centres. Circumstances will vary so much that a single set of rules could be misleading and unnecessarily restrictive.

Instead, principles of management and good practice from a large pool of collective experiences are outlined in this handbook. They should be applied with consideration for individual needs.

There is no single ideal support craft for clubs or teaching centres, although some types come close to the ideal for inland and coastal locations respectively, as detailed below.

With the exception of larger displacement craft used only as "mother ships", every support boat must fulfil certain criteria. It must:

★ contain positive built-in buoyancy
★ have low freeboard to allow access from water
★ be adequately fendered
★ be manoeuvrable at slow speed in strong winds.

The two most popular hull types to meet these requirements are the dory and the rigid-hulled inflatable (RIB). Each has advantages over the other for specific locations, as outlined below, but neither will meet all the requirements of some clubs and centres.

Displacement Craft

Many aspects of support work are best served by larger, strongly built inboard-powered displacement craft. In particular, they suit the following uses:

★ Committee boat, especially at coastal locations
★ Club ferry to keelboat moorings
★ Mother ship for training or expedition fleet
★ Tug for multiple towing.

Typically, such a boat will be of round-bilge design, 6-8m in length, of heavy displacement g.r.p. construction with a water-cooled inboard diesel engine of 12-30 hp. It will either be open, with tiller steering or have a small cabin (cuddy) forward and wheel steering.

It should be equipped with substantial all-round fendering at a suitable height on the hull and have large sturdy cleats or posts both at the bow and at each quarter, or preferably a large samson post amidships.

Quite apart from the obvious benefit of space and capacity, such a craft has the following advantages:

★ Easily driven at displacement speeds
★ Low fuel consumption and hence running costs
★ Good directional stability
★ Performance not greatly affected by load
★ Seakindly motion in bad weather.

Its disadvantages stem from its size and weight:

★ Must be kept afloat
★ Maximum hull speed governed by length
★ Difficult to handle in close quarters manoeuvres
★ Cannot usually be beached
★ Freeboard makes MOB recovery difficult
★ Potential damage alongside capsized dinghies.

Planing Craft

Whilst displacement craft are practical for many purposes, they have the major drawback that they cannot reach casualties at high speed. There are four basic types of planing hulls which can, but they each have their individual advantages and disadvantages.

Inflatables

An inflatable craft used in a support role should be at least 4m overall with a solid floor and an outboard matched to its size. Such inflatables are likely to have sponsons extending beyond the transom, to provide a reserve of buoyancy for carrying larger outboards. These craft are:

★ Very portable and need no trailer
★ Relatively stable at rest
★ Immensely buoyant
★ Capable of carrying considerable loads
★ Able to come alongside other boats without damage
★ Suitable for recovery of people from the water
★ Easily beached.

Unfortunately, they

★ Are affected by strong winds
★ Have low directional stability
★ Give a rough, wet ride at speed
★ Can be relatively short lived
★ Have limitations for towing, except alongside.

These limitations are even more marked in smaller inflatables, hence the minimum size recommended above.

Rigid-hulled Inflatables Boats (RIBs)

This is probably the most versatile type of support craft, particularly for coastal use. It combines most of the good points of inflatables and rigid V-shaped hulls and, size for size, is more seaworthy in heavy weather than the dory.

Its advantages can be summarised as:
★ Good directional stability
★ High buoyancy
★ Exceptional seaworthiness in bad weather
★ High load carrying capacity
★ Soft contact with other boats etc
★ Suitable for recovery of people from the water
★ Can be beached if necessary.

Against these, it:
★ Requires trailer or launching trolley
★ Can be prone to abrasion and damage
★ Can have low initial stability at rest.

To overcome this last problem, some RIBs have a flooding central section in the lower hull which automatically fills with water when the boat is at rest to dampen roll and increase stability.

These types need a build-up period of a few seconds when accelerated from rest to drain the water away. Although this handling characteristic is accepted by all those who favour the RIB for coastal use, it may swing the choice in favour of the dory for confined inland waters.

Dory, Sled or Cathedral Hulls

The dory is undoubtedly the most popular type of support boat for use on inland and sheltered coastal water. This is probably due to the fact that it is both a stable platform when at rest and a fast,

highly manoeuvrable planing craft.

Both these characteristics are a direct function of the distinctive hull shape, in which the displacement is distributed between the sponsons. The ride and performance are helped to some extent by a cushion of air forced under the hull at speed.

To summarise, the advantages are:
★ High stability at rest
★ Good directional stability at low speeds
★ Good load carrying capacity
★ High manoeuvrability at high speeds on flat water
★ Efficient hull shape - good fuel economy
★ Buoyancy usually built in (between skins)
★ Suitable for recovery of people from the water
★ Can be beached.

The disadvantages are:
★ Uncomfortable and wet ride at high speed in waves
★ Requires trailer or launching trolley
★ Hull damage may be difficult to repair.

One particular variation on the hull shape which has become increasing common in sailing centres in recent years is the Commando. It has become popular for the combined role of teaching platform and safety boat for groups of windsurfers or singlehanded dinghies. This is due to its:
★ Rugged spun-polyethylene construction
★ Light weight for launching/beaching
★ Low purchase and operating costs.

Rigid-V Hulls

Since the advent of RIBs, other conventional-hulled powerboats have become rare as support craft. Where they are used, it is because of the following advantages:

★ Longer life expectancy than some inflatables
★ Good directional stability at speed
★ Soft ride at speed (deep V)

Against these must be set the disadvantages of:

★ Poor initial stability at rest
★ Risk of damage when in contact with other boats
★ Requires trailer or launching trolley.

Choice of Engine

The basic decisions about inboard or outboard, petrol or diesel are limited to a great extent by the choice of craft. The most common choices are diesel inboards for displacement craft and petrol outboards for planing craft.

Displacement Craft

For the roles of the displacement craft outlined above, an inboard installation is generally favoured. The only advantages an outboard might have - portability and ease of maintenance - are outweighed by all the advantages of inboards:

★ Slow running, high torque for maximum towing capability
★ Propeller always immersed, especially in waves
★ Low fuel consumption, hence low running costs
★ Permanent installation; low risk of theft.

When choosing between petrol and diesel, it is generally true that petrol engines are cheaper to buy, lighter, quieter and more easily maintained by the amateur mechanic but have a serious fire risk and an electrical ignition system which is a potential source of trouble.

Diesel engines involve a much smaller fire risk, are more reliable and are cheaper to operate. Fuel savings will not outweigh the extra initial cost for some time, however, while diesels are still heavier for a given power, tend to be noisier, smellier, and the fuel injection equipment needs professional maintenance.

The maximum speed of a displacement hull is governed by its waterline length. Attempts to drive it faster will result in greater fuel consumption, a tendency for the stern to squat and an increased wash. Thus there is no point in installing a larger engine to increase performance.

The wave formation created by the boat will limit the boat's speed (V) to about 1.4 x the square root of the waterline length (L). The formula $V/\sqrt{L}$ is called the speed/length ratio and for economical operation should be kept to 1.2 or less.

This means that for a displacement craft of say 16ft l.w.l. the maximum economical speed is 4 x 1.2 = 4.8 knots. Any attempt to drive this boat at a greater speed requires a disproportionate increase in power and hence in fuel consumed for every fraction of a knot achieved.

Planing Craft

With the exception of certain specialised, larger craft which use outdrives, the outboard is the universal choice of power for planing support boats such as RIBs and dories.

Similarly, although diesel outboards are available, the realistic option is petrol, so the choice is simply four-stroke or two-stroke and, if the latter, whether the oil is mixed with the petrol in the tank or injected from a separate reservoir directly into the engine. Manufacturers are quick to point out the comparative advantages, but for many clubs the choice of brand and hence model is governed by the proximity of a dealer for spares and servicing.

Engine power will be within the lower and upper limits given by the boat manufacturer. Each boat needs a certain minimum power to get "over the hump" and start planing. Thereafter, more power means more speed and higher consumption up to the limit for safety.

Every outboard manufacturer now supplies the majority of engines equipped with isolation switches and "kill-cords". These are attached to the coxswain so that the engine will be cut if he falls overboard. The majority of older engines can be modified cheaply to accommodate the switch and cord.

The nightmare of an unmanned powerboat circling at high speed to maim or kill its own coxswain has become real enough for every club or centre to insist that all outboards are fitted with kill-cords and that all crews realise their importance.

In clubs and centres running several outboard support boats, there is a lot to be said for standardisation of engines, with the resulting benefits in:

- ★ Standardisation of fuel mixes and tank connections
- ★ Simpler stocks of spare plugs, propellers etc
- ★ Interchange of engines for repairs and service.

The potential for injury caused by a turning propeller is widely acknowledged, and several centres have tried water-jet engines but they have yet to win widespread acceptance.

As an alternative, in locations where support craft often have to approach people in the water, some centres use shrouded propellers or prop guards. These have an adverse effect both on acceleration and top speed, but apart from the obvious safety factor tend to result in longer propeller life.

SUMMARY OF KEY POINTS

- ★ Dories are the most popular type of support craft for club and centre use inland; RIBs are the most versatile for coastal use.
- ★ There is a role for the displacement craft in most locations, particularly as a mother ship and tug.
- ★ All outboard engines should be fitted with kill-cords, and all crews briefed as to their importance.
- ★ Standardisation of engines aids operation and maintenance programmes.
- ★ Whenever possible, each club or centre should try to have a minimum of two safety boats afloat.

MAINTENANCE PROGRAMMES

The worst thing which can be said about any club boat is that it is owned by everyone and yet owned by no-one.

Ideally, a committee member should be nominated to take overall responsibility for all the support boats. He will organise the maintenance and servicing programmes but that doesn't mean he will do all of the work!

He should, however, prepare operating procedures and checklists to help every Officer of the Day and Safety Boat Crew prepare, use and store the boats with the minimum of fuss. If every user completes a standard "tick-list" before and after going afloat, and enters engine hours and defects in a support boat log, any problems can be rectified promptly.

This follows the pattern adopted at many teaching centres, where the care of support boats and engines is the responsibility of a bosun, but where any problems which cannot be rectified by the instructor using the boat are immediately notified in a defects book.

Standard procedures would cover points such as:

- ★ Where fuel is stored and mixed
- ★ When tanks are refilled
- ★ What equipment is carried
- ★ Where/how emergency equipment is stowed
- ★ How fuel lines are left after use
- ★ Whether engines are run after use to empty carburetters
- ★ Whether engines are washed down with fresh water
- ★ How boats/engines are secured against theft

Some of these may be of minor significance in themselves, but they all contribute to the smooth running of the engines or the boats, and hence the smooth running of the support operation.

For the provision of safety cover to work effectively within any organisation, it must be treated as an integral part of the overall management. Although there are many similarities between the work of sailing clubs and teaching establishments, for this section of the handbook they will be treated separately.

Sailing Clubs

All organised sailing activity within a dinghy club is normally the overall responsibility of the Officer of the Day (OOD). Clubs will clearly vary in their approach to the management of non-competitive activities, but in those clubs where dinghy racing is the principal activity, the OOD is often also the Race Officer (RO). As such, he has overall responsibility for every aspect of the race organisation, from determining the course to presenting the results.

In normal club racing, safety boat crews usually report directly to the OOD. For larger events there is often a more detailed framework of organisation for the Race Team, but it tends to follow the pattern that the Race Officer will, either personally or via a safety co-ordinator, direct the work of safety boat crews.

Although clubs will not normally be under any legal duty to provide safety cover, it has become an accepted part of the sport of dinghy racing that they should do so. Competitors in club races, regattas and open meetings therefore normally look to the organisers to supply suitable safety cover. If such provision exists within a club, then competitors are, (according to our legal advice) reasonably entitled to rely on an effective service.

This does nothing to lessen the fundamental responsibility of every helmsman under the Racing Rules of Sailing:
"A boat is solely responsible for deciding whether or not to start or to continue racing".

So, from a safety angle, regardless of legal liability, adult safety starts with the individual sailors to ensure that their craft are seaworthy, they themselves are properly equipped and all gear is serviceable.

Whilst the majority of dinghy race organisers now require all competitors to wear personal buoyancy in strong conditions, some clubs still only require competitors to carry such personal buoyancy with them in the boat; the decision when to wear it being left to the individual.

Similarly, whilst almost every class association publishes rules on boat buoyancy, it is the owner's, not the club's, responsibility to ensure that his boat complies with these rules.

The net result of all these factors is that the OOD managing club racing events *should* be reassured that the competitors are competent to sail, are complying with any club rules about personal buoyancy and are sailing boats which will remain buoyant.

His overall approach to the safety of any event will be to decide whether his safety team can deal with most likely emergencies, including the fact in marginal weather that inexperienced and younger competitors might choose to sail in conditions which are beyond their capabilities.

In such conditions, he may have a responsibility to advise inexperienced and younger sailors that they might have difficulty and therefore should not compete.

When weather conditions are such that the available safety cover is considered inadequate for the predicted capability of competitors, the OOD has a responsibility either to postpone or abandon the event or otherwise restrict activity to within the capabilities of the safety team.

In making this decision, the OOD will take account of many factors including the way competitors are clothed and the expected duration of bad weather.

In all conditions, the OOD will specify the priorities and tactical positioning of safety boats. In theory, he will also have to brief safety boat crews on their task, including how to deal with occasions when they should over-ride the wishes of dinghy crews who have indicated that they do not wish to receive help but who are deemed to be in need of urgent attention.

The basic responsibility of the safety boat crew is to ensure that the instructions of the OOD or RO are carried out. The single most important part of this responsibility is to attend every capsize, probably only briefly and sometimes at a distance, to count heads, check that the crew are not injured and need no further assistance.

One of the major sources of friction at club and open events is that this responsibility is sometimes taken too zealously by over-enthusiastic safety boat crews, to the annoyance of helmsmen who simply want to right their boats and continue racing. This friction can be overcome if all competitors are made aware of the club's standing procedures for safety boat crews.

Teaching Establishments

In many ways the task of providing safety cover for students under instruction is much easier than for racing crews, but all of these are outweighed by the far greater responsibility of dealing with novices, rather than experienced sailors.

Any experienced sailor is deemed to accept the ordinary perils of the sea and thus cannot complain of injury or damage if he voluntarily accepts the risks of sailing. It is neatly summed up by the lawyers' phrase "Volenti non fit injuria".

Totally different considerations arise where children and novices are concerned. Neither could be expected to assume a risk associated with the sport voluntarily because they cannot appreciate the inherent dangers. Thus every teaching establishment must provide a safe framework of operation which includes the provision to deal with all eventualities on the water.

In providing this framework, the task of the Principal or Chief Instructor is made easier by the fact that he can and should control the sailing area, the length of the session and the instructor/ student ratio when necessary to keep things under control. Decisions about each of these will be made on the spot by the person directly responsible for each group.

Due to the very nature of their role, students expect to be told what to do by instructors regarding their sailing, and so there is likely to be compliance with any decision to go ashore or for the whole session to be abandoned.

The practical difficulties for those providing safety cover within a teaching establishment usually arise because the students, whether dinghy sailors or windsurfers, cannot be relied upon to provide any self-help. Add to that the fact that problems tend to occur not just to one student but to the whole group simultaneously and you have the background to the "epic" which is within the experience of most seasoned instructors.

SUMMARY OF KEY POINTS

★ Safety cover within clubs usually comes under the responsibility of the Officer of the Day, but may be delegated to a co-ordinator.
★ Club safety boat crews must be briefed on when to intervene in an incident for the safety of the sailors involved.
★ Standing procedures for dealing with rescues should be made widely known to avoid conflict.

Sailing Clubs

As outlined above, club safety boat crews are normally responsible to the Race Officer or OOD, who will specify priorities and operating areas.

The priorities are never in doubt:
1. Safety of crews being rescued
2. Safety of other crews
3. Prevention of further damage to disabled boats and windsurfers
4. Recovery of disabled or capsized boats and windsurfers.

These priorities also indicate the responsibility of safety boat crews towards club members. As would be expected, life always comes before property.

The principal danger with inexperienced safety boat crews is their unwitting failure to remember this basic rule. It usually occurs when a crew is so deeply involved with recovering one capsized boat that they fail to keep an adequate look-out for the rest of the fleet. Once the crew of a dinghy or windsurfer have been rescued and brought aboard the safety boat, that incident may suddenly switch from priority 1 to 4, because of what is happening elsewhere.

There are occasions when other calls are made on safety boats and their crews. For example, a mark might have dragged and need re-laying or the club Press Officer might want a close-up photograph of the racing for Yachts & Yachting or the local newspaper.

On such occasions the safety boat crew should always consult the OOD before deviating from their primary role. Even if approval is given, crews should always be prepared to abandon whatever they are doing to deal with a rescue.

Teaching Establishments

Within the majority of teaching establishments, safety cover is an integral part of the teaching operation. In the case of virtually all singlehanded dinghy teaching, improvers and advanced courses in two-man boats and some windsurfing instruction, the instructor often mans a boat which combines the role of teaching platform and safety boat.

In such instances, the instructor is responsible for the safety of his group to the Chief Instructor. Details of group activities, operating area and length of session will have been agreed in advance.

The alternative pattern for such teaching is that the instructor himself sails one of the dinghies or boards, with separate safety cover either dedicated to the teaching group or shared with other, similar groups operating in the same area. In such cases, the safety boat crews have a responsibility to the instructor(s) not to leave the water until all students are ashore.

When safety boats are shared between two groups, there must be an agreed signal to abandon the sailing for both groups if the safety cover becomes so involved in one rescue that it cannot continue to provide cover.

In much the same way, teaching in larger dinghies usually operates on the basis of an instructor in each boat with two or three students, with separate safety boat cover for the group. Although the general principle that the safety boat crew is responsible to the group instructor still applies, it is usually an academic point, because it tends to be the group instructor who mans the safety boat!

SUMMARY OF KEY POINTS
★ People before property.
★ When dealing with one incident, safety boat crews should keep a watch on the rest of the craft in their group or zone.
★ The safety boat crew's responsibility ends only when all craft are ashore.

Before dealing with manning and roles in detail, it is worth outlining the overall role of a safety boat crew when arriving at any incident. The first task is to make an assessment and decide into which of the following categories the incident comes:

1. Immediate rescue is needed
2. There is no immediate danger to life, but the safety boat should stand by until the sailors have brought themselves back to a safe condition
3. There is no danger to life or safety, and the safety boat can depart immediately to other incidents.

Of these, the most common will be the second. The very presence of a safety boat nearby is sometimes enough of a morale boost to encourage dinghy sailors or windsurfers to effect a self-rescue.

To emphasise the point made above, when standing by any such incident, a good lookout should always be kept for other craft.

If the incident is assessed as coming into the first category, prompt, decisive action must be taken, following the principles given in Part Two of this book. If the incident comes into the third category, the safety boat should depart immediately, with the crew satisfied that they were on the spot had help been needed.

Sailing Clubs

There should always be at least two people crewing a club rescue boat. Although there are a few "loners" who prefer to work on their own, they would be hard-pressed to do the following:

★ Lift an unconscious person into the safety boat
★ Perform resuscitation whilst returning ashore
★ Right an inverted dinghy with the crew trapped inside.

Quite apart from these extreme examples, all the routine work of the club safety boat is accomplished much more easily with a crew of two and such crewing provides the opportunity for seasoned coxswains to give additional training to less experienced crews. In addition, it is virtually impossible for one person to keep a lookout for others while dealing with an incident.

At least one of the crew, preferably both, should be ready to enter the water if necessary. The roles would normally be defined as coxswain and crew, with the more experienced of the pair being clearly in charge throughout an operation.

Teaching Establishments

In contrast to the crewing of club safety boats, single manning is common practice in dinghy and windsurfer teaching. Although not ideal, the system works because of a number of significant differences between the roles of club and teaching establishment.

The different approach reflects the different activity afloat and the greater control over that activity exercised by those responsible for safety cover. Unlike a club OOD, the Chief Instructor of a teaching establishment can alter the scale (and hence risk) of the activity, quickly and at will.

In addition, the overall ratio of safety cover to the fleet is likely to be much higher, those manning the safety/teaching boats are likely to be full-time staff experienced in dealing with the majority of common problems afloat and, at most centres, additional safety boat crew members are immediately available from the instructors either teaching in dinghies or working in other support boats. Thus although the instructor manning a safety/ teaching boat on his own would be hard pressed to do the three tasks outlined, he is working in an environment where additional experienced help is likely to be immediately at hand.

SUMMARY OF KEY POINTS

★ Club safety boats should be manned by at least two people.
★ At least one person in every safety boat should be prepared to enter the water.

Communication afloat can be considered in three sections: the ability of participants to communicate with support boats; that of support boat crews to communicate with participants, and that of support boat crews to communicate with each other and with the shore base.

Communication from participants

In general, the only effective long-range communication is a visual one. The sight of an inverted dinghy or a windsurfer who continually fails to get started is a clear enough indication, but everyone who goes afloat should be equipped with the means of attracting attention in a less dramatic way, such as:

★ The internationally recognised signal of slowly raising and lowering both outstretched arms
★ The orange square flag available from RYA Windsurfing
★ An agreed local signal, such as the lowering of the mainsail.

It should be noted that the use of distress flares has been omitted only because these comments refer specifically to organised group activities with inherent safety cover.

Communication to participants

Support boats will not normally have to acknowledge a request for assistance - their attendance will speak for itself.

For effective verbal communication between support boats and individual dinghy sailors or windsurfers, three simple principles should be followed:

★ Never try to shout instructions from a moving powerboat. It is far more effective to get in close, cut the engine (or at least throttle down and shift into neutral) and then speak at a reasonable volume.
★ Reduce the actual number of words to the minimum. Before saying anything, think what you need to say and rehearse it in your head; you'll probably find that by simplifying it you can say what you need using only a third of your original words.
★ Always ask for an acknowledgement. In teaching establishments the preliminary briefing for singlehanded groups normally includes the comment "Whenever you receive an instruction from someone in a teaching/safety boat, please acknowledge that you have understood". It is a principle which could effectively be adopted by sailing clubs, too.

Communication within the team

The widespread use of radio, either on Citizens Band (CB) or marine-band VHF, has transformed the area of communication between support boats and their bases.

Part Three of this handbook deals with the subject in more detail; it is obviously in the interests of every club and teaching establishment to ensure that as many people as possible know how to use the equipment and are properly licensed.

SUMMARY OF KEY POINTS

★ Everyone who goes afloat should know the international signals for indicating when assistance is required.
★ Trying to shout instructions from a moving powerboat is pointless. Get in close, stop and speak clearly.
★ If radios are available, everyone who might use them should be trained in the correct voice procedures.

Success in a rescue often depends on the safety boat crew knowing exactly what to do and doing it quickly. Delay often makes things worse.

Safety boat crews should never have to think about which bend or hitch to use when securing towlines or making a boat secure.

Most of the necessary ropework will already be familiar to the experienced sailor or windsurfer, but the correct use of a heaving line will probably be a new technique which needs to be practised.

The heaving line itself can be of three-strand or braided rope, but it must be soft, or pliable. Ropes sold as heaving lines are usually brightly coloured, either 15m or 30m in length, with a "monkey's fist" at one end to aid throwing.

Before throwing, one end must be made fast to the safety boat, not to the thrower.

The line should then be coiled right handed (assuming conventional lay) into the throwing hand, with coils of about 0.5m diameter. The coils are then divided into two, with between a third and a half in the throwing hand.

The throw should be made with a round-arm action, keeping the arm straight. As the throw is made, the non-throwing hand is opened to allow the line to run out.

One neat alternative to coiling is to keep the line stowed in a 'throw-bag'.

Finally, remember that the function of a heaving line is simply that. As it is light enough to throw, it may well not be strong enough for anything more.

It should be used to establish contact with, for example, a dinghy on a lee shore so that a heavier tow line can then be attached to it and run between the dinghy and safety boat.

The preparation for providing safety boat cover includes not only the boat and its equipment but also the crew. The first stage of crew preparation is the training required to do the job; it is recommended that all safety boat crews complete either the Level 2 or Safety Boat Course.

Clothing and Personal Comfort

Choosing the right clothing for safety boat duty can be much more difficult than for the activities which the safety boat crew are supporting. The following considerations should be borne in mind:

★ Length of time afloat
★ The need for at least one crew member to be prepared to enter the water
★ The fact that the duty might involve long periods of inactivity in cold conditions
★ The need for agility in and around the boat.

Every crew member must wear personal buoyancy when afloat. Buoyancy aids allow more mobility than lifejackets, but the latter provide more buoyancy if the crew needs to support another person in the water.

A safety boat crew will only work efficiently if they are comfortable. Hot drinks on cold days and vice versa will aid efficiency.

The Boat

Preparation of the boat itself for safety purposes differs little from that for any other purpose, but remember the following:

★ Anchor and warp suitable for all likely contingencies, including lee shore work
★ Alternative means of propulsion
★ Reserve fuel (high consumption when towing)
★ Neat stowage of heaving line, warps and towlines ready for immediate use
★ Provision of bridle at stern for towline.

Equipment

Safety boat equipment comes into two categories; that needed for the boat itself and that associated with the task. A comprehensive list is given in Part Three, but this could be regarded as excessive for work in very restricted areas and should be modified as appropriate to the location. A minimum standard is included in the specification for a school or club safety boat also given in Part Three.

When equipment is stored away from the boat, it may be convenient to transport and stow it in a container which can quickly be located in position. Examples include the large plastic trays used by bakers for deliveries, plastic milk crates suitably modified and the small plastic dustbins used for home brewing.

Several items of equipment will need watertight stowage and all items should be secured in place. Heaving lines, spare warps and the main towline should all be coiled and secured with buntline hitches, unless stored on a drum.

SUMMARY OF KEY POINTS

★ Dress for comfort and agility in the prevailing conditions.
★ Think through each aspect of the expected tasks. Carry appropriate equipment for the task and area.
★ Familiarise yourself with the use of all equipment.

The ultimate goal of anyone operating a powerboat in a support role should be for their boat handling skills to be second nature, such that they don't have to think about how to put the boat in any position but can simply do it. In that way, support boat crews can concentrate on their task.

That's the goal, but for those who don't quite get there, it's worth looking at the other extreme - the minimum standard acceptable. If those in charge of support boats are not experienced in their work, they are likely to be more of a hazard than a help to sailors and windsurfers in trouble. That implies a clear need for the pattern of gaining experience by an apprenticeship, crewing for experienced coxswains until suffecient boat handling skills in support operations are mastered.

Different craft have a wide range of handling characteristics, affected by underwater shape, method of propulsion, rudder position and size, windage and loading. Nobody can be expected to step into an unfamiliar boat and operate it to its full potential immediately, so a period of familiarity with any boat is an essential part of the preparation for its use.

Single Screw Displacement Craft with Rudder

In a craft steered by rudder, the rudder itself has no effect on steering unless water is flowing past it. This movement of water is obvious when the craft is moving, but the rudder becomes less and less effective as the craft slows down.

The key to low speed manoeuvrability lies in the fact that the rudder is situated immediately astern of the propeller, and hence operates in its slipstream. The boat can be turned even when stationary if a stream of water is pushed over the rudder by giving a burst of power ahead. The same effect will not be evident when the engine is running astern, when the "paddle wheel" effect is more pronounced.
In simple terms, this effect is due to the propeller having a greater efficiency at the bottom of its turning circle than at the top. Although the propeller is pushing the boat ahead or astern through the water, it also acts like a paddle wheel and tries to drive the stern sideways.

Most single-screw boats have right-handed propellers (i.e. they revolve clockwise when viewed from aft). When starting to go ahead from rest, a right-handed propeller kicks the stern of the boat to starboard and the bow swings to port. Going ahead, the effect is not very pronounced, because the stream of water over the rudder has a far stronger influence.

The opposite happens when you start off astern. With a right-handed prop, the stern kicks to port, and the bow swings to starboard. This time, the effect is much more noticeable, especially in boats fitted with large, three bladed propellers.

The combination of propwash over the rudder when going ahead and paddle wheel effect when going astern can be used to minimise the turning circle of a boat in a small space, but you need to know which way to turn.

There are two easy ways of establishing whether you have a right- or left-handed propeller. The first is simply to look at the propeller shaft when the engine is running in gear. When viewed from astern, if the shaft rotates clockwise when running ahead, you have a right-handed propeller, and vice versa.

Assuming you can't easily get access to the prop shaft, the alternative is simply to put the engine into gear astern when securely moored alongside, and see where the turbulence is created. A right-handed propeller going astern will create a wash on the starboard quarter of the boat, and vice versa.

Now you know which way to turn in the smallest possible space, using both ahead and astern gear. With a right-handed propeller, it's better to turn to starboard.

Starting from rest, put the wheel or tiller hard over so that the rudder is to starboard

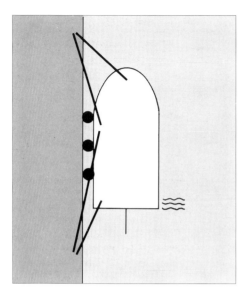

With the boat secured alongside, the direction of propeller rotation can be found by putting the engine into astern gear and looking for the propwash. In this case, the propeller is right-handed

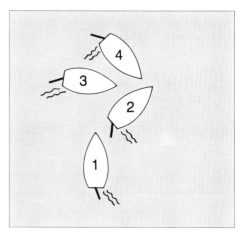

With a right-handed propeller, the tightest turn using both gears will be made to starboard. From rest, the helm is put hard to starboard and a burst of power ahead is given (1). As soon as the boat starts to move forward, power astern (2) will stop it but swing the stern further to port. The sequence is repeated (3 & 4) as often as needed to complete the turn. Remember to pause in neutral before each gear change

and leave it there. A burst of power ahead will swing the stern to port before the boat starts moving ahead. As soon as it does so, come back into neutral, pause, then give a burst of power astern, causing the stern to be kicked further to port. As soon as the boat starts to move astern, come back into neutral, pause and then repeat the whole procedure.

With practice, it is possible to turn many displacement boats in little more than their own length in this way without touching the helm. It is essential to pause in neutral between each gear change to avoid damage to the gearbox.

In contrast, turn to port if you want to do a normal turn of 180 degrees from rest in a boat equipped with a right-handed propeller, without going astern. You will find that the boat will turn a tighter circle to port because the initial kick of the propeller when starting from rest swings the bow in that direction.

Displacement craft tend to turn about a pivot point which, when going ahead, is usually about a third of the length aft. You

must be aware of this when manoeuvring in close quarters, and allow for the stern to swing out of the turn. Going astern, the pivot point moves towards the stern and so the bow will swing out of the turn.

In strong winds, the windage of the hull may cause handling problems, particularly if the boat is fitted with a cuddy forwards. When the boat is stationary, the bow will quickly blow off downwind and keeping station may be difficult.

Moving astern, the effect will be even more pronounced, due to the pivot point being well aft. The combination of windage and paddle wheel effect make it impossible to manoeuvre some displacement craft slowly astern in certain directions, as the following example shows.

In the diagram, the committee boat is to be berthed to leeward of the jetty and stern to the shore, but cannot reach the jetty by manoeuvring slowly astern from her present position, because the bow is being blown off downwind and the stern will be pushed to port.

That leaves three options:

★   Motor in astern fast enough to

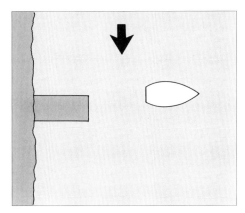

Displacement boats may be difficult to handle slowly astern in strong winds (see text)

overcome windage and stop at the last minute by going ahead
★   Motor to a position head to wind and upwind of the jetty so that a controlled approach astern may be made, taking account of windage and paddle wheel effect
★   Motor in ahead, secure alongside and warp the boat round.
Clearly the first two options require very confident boat handling and are prone to problems, so the third should never be dismissed if you have doubts about the boat's characteristics.

Outboards and Outdrives

Steering with an outboard differs from inboard craft because the leg which holds the propeller in the water pivots under the action of the steering wheel or tiller to direct the propeller thrust in the required direction and there is no other rudder.The paddlewheel effect is virtually negligible in vessels equipped with outboards or outdrives because of the propeller characteristics.

Outboards and outdrives have very positive steering when the propeller is being driven either ahead or astern but very little steering when the engine is in neutral. It is also important to note that when going astern with this form of steering the pivot point of the boat is brought a very long way aft and so the bow will swing well out of the turn.

When manoeuvring outboard or outdrive powered boats in close quarters, make sure that the correct helm is applied before engaging ahead or astern gear. With this type of propulsion a helm indicator at the steering position is useful.

When operating smaller outboard powered craft with tiller steering, it should be possible for the helmsman to sit on the opposite side of the boat to the tiller, steering with his tiller arm across the front of the engine.

Not only will this be a more comfortable position, but it enables the helmsman to apply full lock either way without the tiller being obstructed by his body or caught in his clothing. As the gear shift is usually on the opposite side to the tiller, it also means that he can change gear more easily.

When manoeuvring such boats astern, it is best to stand up and face astern, with the tiller in one hand and the gear shift in the other. Steering then becomes obvious, but the helmsman must not forget to watch the swing of the bow from time to time.

High speed manoeuvring

The only time high speed manoeuvres are used within a support role are to reach the scene of trouble or to get injured sailors ashore. The safety boat coxswain who spends his whole duty rushing around the course will earn nothing but contempt from the people for whom he is providing safety cover and embarrassment for those who are supervising his activities.

Thus the high speed handling skills needed by the support boat coxswain are no more than those included in Level 2 of the National Powerboat Scheme. These are detailed in the G20 logbook but two points are sufficiently important to justify repetition.

The first is that engine isolation keys (kill-cords or jack-plugs) should be fitted to all high-speed outboard powered craft and used as appropriate. Enough injuries have been caused already within our sport to confirm the lethal potential of a high-powered craft out of control.

The second is that the coxswain should keep his hand on the throttle throughout any high speed handling, so that he can react instantly to the boat's motion in waves.

The only additional point to introduce in this context is the need to keep any rescued sailors low in the safety boat, particularly those who have been in the water for long, to reduce any further heat loss while they are being taken ashore.

Handling Under Oars

There will be times when every safety boat coxswain has to manoeuvre his boat under oars or paddles. Not only do they provide very precise manoeuvring in close quarters and the ability to keep station, but in certain circumstances give the only safe means of approaching someone in the water.

The techniques of rowing - or the sculling and drawstrokes needed for paddles - should be within the repertoire of anyone who calls himself a competent powerboat handler.

Tactical Positioning

Tactical positioning of safety boats is governed by one major physiological factor. It is widely acknowledged that permanent brain damage can occur if the brain is deprived of oxygen for more than three minutes. The most likely cause in our sport will be when a dinghy sailor or windsurfer is unconscious, face down, in the water and it therefore provides a useful yardstick for safety boat cover.

Given the requirement to attend every capsize within three minutes, it follows that some thought should be given to tactical positioning by safety boats at racing events. It is of rather less importance at teaching establishments where, due to the dual-role of support boats, they are likely to be working in close proximity to their whole group.

As outlined earlier, the club OOD may well designate specific zones of operation for individual boat crews, the size of each zone being governed by boat type and speed. It is obviously impossible in this handbook to give specific guidance to suit all areas, but OODs are likely to consider the following factors:

★ In strong winds and high waves it will be easier for the safety boat crew to observe a racing fleet from upwind

★ In such conditions it will also be easier and faster to travel cross- or downwind rather than upwind

★ The most likely capsize location is the gybe mark

★ The leg of the course most prone to capsize is a dead run

★ Collisions are most likely during the period from immediately before the start to the end of the first beat.

The leg of the course most prone to capsize is the dead run

Tactical positioning of displacement craft will depend on their role. If, as is likely, they are acting simply as towing or mother ships, they should be located at fixed, known points around the course and should return to these points as soon as possible after each incident. In that way, they will act as natural collecting points.

Coming Alongside Other Craft

The general principles of coming alongside a jetty, pier or another boat are covered at Level 2 in the Scheme. They can be summarised as:

- ★ Assessment - is it safe? Which side?
- ★ Preparation - warps, fenders
- ★ Approach - direction and speed, escape route
- ★ Securing - use of warps, cleats

With the exception of the need to come alongside a disabled craft in order to take it into tow, the common reasons for a support boat to come alongside another craft all involve a very short-term manoeuvre. It might be the need to take an instructor out of a dinghy to enable the students to sail solo, or to assess a minor injury during a club race. Either way, it calls for a different technique to that required for coming alongside a stationary object.

If possible, the dinghy crew should be asked to slow down by lying-to or heaving-to. The support boat can then come alongside to windward, where its crew will be clear of flogging sails and a swinging boom. The dinghy should not be instructed to slow down by going head to wind, as this position is virtually impossible to maintain for long and the reaction of the boat will be unpredictable.

Approaching Capsized Craft

As outlined in Part One, it is quite often appropriate for a safety boat to stand by rather than to intervene immediately. The right position will be within earshot but not placed so that dinghy and safety boat will drift together.

If approaching a dinghy which is capsized to 90 degrees and clearly in need of immediate assistance, the safest line will be towards the forestay, as shown.

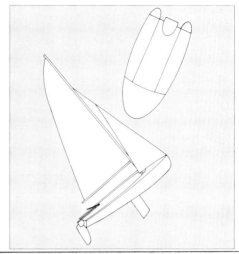

Approaching a capsized dinghy

This allows the safety boat crew to prevent full inversion without any risk of damage to crew or boat from the mast acting as a lance, whilst it also keeps the engine clear of the dinghy sails and crew.

The alternative is to put the safety boat alongside the capsized hull so that the crew can right it by levering down on the centreboard in the conventional way.

When approaching a fully inverted dinghy, it is best to come alongside so that both bows are pointing in the same direction. This means that when the boat has been righted to 90 degrees, it can easily be manoeuvred head to wind before being fully righted.

Mark Laying and Recovery

There is no mystique to the task of mark laying and recovery, which should be treated according to exactly the same principles as anchoring.

The most common faults arise from:

- ★ Lack of preparation - marks should be ready such that the anchor or weight is dropped first, then the line paid out smoothly as required, with the mark itself and its sinker being dropped last
- ★ Poor appreciation of wind or tide - dropping the anchor where you want the mark to be is doomed to disappointment.

★ Failure to adjust the length of line to depth of water - the usual result of this is a mess of rope floating close to the mark in just the right place to trap unwary centreboards or daggerboards.

Even the best mark-boat crews, directed at world championships by Race Officers aided by radar and Decca, get it wrong occasionally, so don't be disheartened. The quick way to reposition a mark in deep water without having to haul in all the line is to retrieve the mark itself and its sinker, haul in a little of the line and then motor the anchor or weight to where it is needed by trawling it along the seabed.

Rescue of Personnel in the Water

Left to the end of this section to emphasise its importance, this topic could alternatively be considered as the start of the following section on dinghy rescue.

The approach to a person in the water should be treated in exactly the same way as a man overboard, the key point being that the recovery is made with the engine switched off. The only possible exception to this is if the recovery attempt is being made in such a location that the risk of the engine not re-starting again would put the safety boat crew themselves, as well as the MOB, into grave and imminent danger.

The direction of approach in an emergency is slightly less critical than when performing the same manoeuvre in a sailing dinghy but it is still preferable to make the final approach from downwind, so that speed can be controlled more readily. The alternative, an approach from upwind, could result in such close contact with the MOB that serious injuries are caused.

The person could be picked up on either side of the boat, the coxswain choosing the side which gives better visibility and fewer obstructions. The actual technique of recovering an unconscious person from the water depends on the type of boat but normally needs two people.

The ideal method can be performed from an inflatable or RIB. The casualty should be turned with his back to the boat. Crew members positioned either side of him can get their arms right underneath his armpits. He can then be lifted aboard.

This technique has the advantage that the casualty's airway is kept open as he is hauled backwards into the boat and his legs will tend to drift away from the boat, making recovery easier.

To avoid the risk of back injury in hard-sided boats such as dories, the alternative method is to bring the casualty in facing towards the boat. An attempt must be made to maintain an open airway while this is being done. The disadvantage of this technique is the likelihood of the casualty's legs swinging under the boat and making recovery more difficult. The technique should be a lift, followed by turning the casualty onto his back.

Once in the boat, resuscitation can be given given most easily if the casualty is lying across the thwart, or sponsons.

If the recovery of a person in the water has to be made from a larger, displacement boat, the safest procedure is to stand off, throw a line to the person and pull him in on that line. If he is unconscious, recovery from a boat with high freeboard might depend on sending one of the crew into the water (attached to a line) for retrieval.

When returning ashore with an unconscious casualty, he should be put in the recovery position, preferably with his head towards the stern and as far aft as possible to reduce further injury caused by the boat's motion. Careful check must be maintained to ensure that his face is clear of any water in the boat.

SUMMARY OF KEY POINTS

★ Practise close-quarters boat handling to gain familiarity with your safety boat.
★ In high-speed craft, wear the kill-cord.
★ Attend every capsize within three minutes, if only to check the crew are safe and establish that you are not needed.
★ In multiple incidents, attend to all people before dealing with any craft.
★ Approach people in the water from downwind.
★ Cut the engine when dealing with people in the water.

RYA Membership

Promoting and Protecting Boating
www.rya.org.uk

RYA *Membership*

Promoting and Protecting Boating

The RYA is the national organisation which represents the interests of everyone who goes boating for pleasure.

The greater the membership, the louder our voice when it comes to protecting members' interests.

Apply for membership today, and support the RYA, to help the RYA support you.

Benefits of Membership

- Access to expert advice on all aspects of boating from legal wrangles to training matters
- Special members' discounts on a range of products and services including boat insurance, books, videos and class certificates
- Free issue of certificates of competence, increasingly asked for by everyone from overseas governments to holiday companies, insurance underwriters to boat hirers

- Access to the wide range of RYA publications, including the quarterly magazine
- Third Party insurance for windsurfing members
- Free Internet access with RYA-Online
- Special discounts on AA membership
- Regular offers in RYA Magazine
- ...and much more

Join now - membership form opposite

Join online at *www.rya.org.uk*

Visit our website for information, advice, members' services and web shop.

1 Important

To help us comply with Data Protection legislation, please tick *either* Box A or Box B (you must tick Box A to ensure you receive the full benefits of RYA membership). The RYA will not pass your data to third parties.

- [ ] **A.** I wish to join the RYA and receive future information on member services, benefits (as listed in RYA Magazine and website) and offers.
- [ ] **B.** I wish to join the RYA but do not wish to receive future information on member services, benefits (as listed in RYA Magazine and website) and offers.

When completed, please send this form to: RYA, RYA House, Ensign Way, Hamble, Southampton, SO31 4YA

2

Title	Forename	Surname	Date of Birth		Male	Female
			D D / M M / Y Y			
1.						
2.			D D / M M / Y Y			
3.			D D / M M / Y Y			
4.			D D / M M / Y Y			

Address

Town   **County**   **Post Code**

Evening Telephone   **Daytime Telephone**

email

Signature: _____ Date: _____

3 Type of membership required: *(Tick Box)*

- [ ] **Personal** *Current full annual rate £33 or £30 by Direct Debit*
- [ ] **Under 21** *Current full annual rate £11 (no reduction for Direct Debit)*
- [ ] **Family*** *Current full annual rate £50 or £47 by Direct Debit*

* *Family Membership: 2 adults plus any under 21s all living at the same address*

Please see Direct Debit form overleaf

4 Please tick ONE box to show your main boating interest.

[ ] Yacht Racing	[ ] Yacht Cruising
[ ] Dinghy Racing	[ ] Dinghy Cruising
[ ] Personal Watercraft	[ ] Inland Waterways
[ ] Powerboat Racing	[ ] Windsurfing
[ ] Motor Boating	[ ] Sportsboats and RIBs

RYA Instructions to your Bank or Building Society to pay by Direct Debit

Please complete this form and return it to:
Royal Yachting Association, RYA House, Ensign Way, Hamble, Southampton, Hampshire SO31 4YA

DIRECT Debit

To The Manager: Bank/Building Society

Address:

Post Code:

2. Name(s) of account holder(s)

3. Branch Sort Code

☐☐ — ☐☐ — ☐☐

4. Bank or Building Society account number

☐☐☐☐☐☐☐☐

Banks and Building Societies may not accept Direct Debit instructions for some types of account

Cash, Cheque, Postal Order enclosed £ ☐
Made payable to the Royal Yachting Association

077   **Office use only:** Membership Number Allocated ☐

Originators Identification Number

9	5	5	2	1	3

5. RYA Membership Number (For office use only)

6. Instruction to pay your Bank or Building Society

Please pay Royal Yachting Association Direct Debits from the account detailed in this instruction subject to the safeguards assured by The Direct Debit Guarantee.
I understand that this instruction may remain with the Royal Yachting Association and, if so, details will be passed electronically to my Bank/Building Society.

Signature(s) _____

Date _____

Office use / Centre Stamp

Despite the title, this section will start and end with comments about non-rescue.

If a dinghy crew is still capable, the first stage of assistance given by a safety boat crew should be verbal, rather than physical. It may simply be that the dinghy sailors need a little encouragement to do the right things, while their morale will be boosted by the presence of the safety boat.

Similarly, the first stage of intervention could be quite literally to lend a helping hand, with extra leverage on the centreboard or mast to assist with righting. This could be followed by holding the dinghy stable for long enough for the crew to get back aboard and prepare for sailing.

Once you have decided that full intervention is needed, the first stage is to get the dinghy crew out of the water and into the safety boat. At best, that gives you extra help; at worst, it keeps them out of further danger.

Righting Capsized Craft

As outlined above, if a quick helping hand is all that is needed, the best approach is towards the the forestay. The safety boat crew can then "walk the mast up" towards the hull, which is usually all the extra righting moment needed to assist the dinghy crew.

Alternatively, if the safety boat can be brought alongside the dinghy without risk of damage, the approach should be beside the centreboard, with both bows facing in the same direction. The dinghy can then be righted in the conventional way, the safety boat providing a stable platform for the crew to exert leverage either via the centreboard or jib sheet over the hull.

It may also help both of these techniques if the safety boat coxswain can manoeuvre the bow of the capsized dinghy into the wind, since this eases the pressure of the wind on the sails and of the waves on the hull.

In heavy conditions, it is easier to right the dinghy after the sails have been lowered, especially if a spinnaker was being flown before the capsize. If the dinghy crew are still in the water, they should release the halyards and gather in the sails; if not, one of the safety boat crew will probably have to enter the water in order to reach the appropriate cleats.

Righting Inverted Boats

Inversions fall into one of three categories:

★ in deep waters with the mast clear of the bottom
★ in shallow water with the mast just touching the bottom
★ in slightly deeper water with the mast well jammed in the bottom.

If the dinghy is in deep water, the first action should be to come alongside to leeward and try to sink the leeward quarter in the conventional way to bring the boat into the 90 degree capsize position, then proceed as above.

If that fails, try taking a jibsheet over the dinghy, behind the centreboard (if it is still out), then stand on the gunwhale or kneel on the bilge and pull! You may need to attach a long line to the sheet or even fix a line with a carbine hook to the shroud and lead that over the hull.

If the dinghy just slides sideways, pull the bow round into the wind and try again. Another, more drastic, method which has proved effective is to take the painter or attach a line at the bow and start towing the dinghy slowly. This should "screw" the boat into the 90 degree capsize position.

In water which is too shallow for a complete inversion, it is always better to get the dinghy crew into the safety boat. The worst place they can be is actually on the dinghy hull, where their weight will be help to embed the mast in the bottom.

The greatest danger when trying to recover a dinghy from a partial inversion is that of bending or even breaking the mast. To avoid this, ensure that any pull you make is as nearly as possible in line with the mast.

This can be done most quickly by fixing

a line to the shroud. Better alternatives, although they take slightly longer to set up, are to secure a line to a strong point, such as the thwart, and then lead it through the centreboard case or make a bridle from bow to stern.

Once you have a suitable line attached, apply the pull by moving gently off parallel to the mast. You should then be in a position to take the safety boat round to the forestay and continue as above.

Righting Singlehanders

Capsizes are commonplace among many singlehanded teaching groups and as fatigue sets in, so the students' ability to cope will quickly decrease. Time spent in the water must be kept to a minimum so prompt action is vital.

One of the quickest and most effective forms of help is for the safety boat to make the same approach as in the diagram and "walk the mast up". The safety boat crew can then help to hold the dinghy upright while the crew climbs aboard and gets sorted out.

Singlehanders respond well to righting from inversion in all the ways outlined above; in a teaching establishment students should be briefed not to secure their painters around the mast but leave them lying along the foredeck, so that they can quickly be grabbed by the safety boat crew when necessary.

The majority of popular singlehanders come up nearly dry after capsize; Optimists are the exception and in the unlikely event of capsize might need further attention after righting to help the young helmsman bail out.

Righting Multihulls

Multihulls now account for about 10% of the dinghy classes and, with the exception of the Challenger trimaran, all the common ones are catamarans; the following comments therefore apply specifically to cats.

The biggest danger after a multihull capsize is of the crew becoming separated from the boat, due to the high windage and hence high downwind speed of the capsized cat.

Although the general principles of recovery follow those for monohulls, the following points are worthy of special note:

★ Sheets and traveller must be released before righting
★ After 90 degree capsize, approach the forestay and walk the mast up
★ After inversion, go alongside to leeward and pass a line right over both hulls, around the windward hull attach it to the main beam. With the cat crew positioned at the stern of the leeward hull, motor very gently away to pull the cat up to the 90 degree position.

Lee Shore Operations

Unless you are very confident of your boat handling, the best way of retrieving a dinghy from a lee shore is to anchor off and then veer down on your anchor warp until you can throw a heaving-line. Once a tow

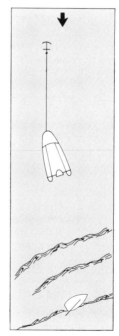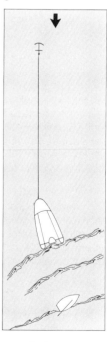

The only safe way to recover a dinghy on a lee shore in surf is to anchor well outside the surf line and veer the safety boat down until just clear of the surf line before throwing or drifting a heaving line ashore

line has been secured to the dinghy, the safety boat can then haul in on its anchor warp until both vessels are in deep water.

This method is the only seamanlike manoeuvre in coastal areas with heavy surf, where it may be impossible to turn the safety boat in waves to clear the shore. In such conditions, the safety boat should be anchored well clear of the surf line and warp veered out until the boat is just clear of the surf.

On flat water inland, particularly large reservoirs where anchoring is totally impractical, a different approach is required.

The general principle is to:
★ go in close enough to throw a heaving line without endangering the safety boat
★ secure a tow line from the dinghy to the stern of the safety boat
★ motor ahead directly to windward to get both boats clear.

It is usually not practical for the safety boat to motor towards the shore, pass the line and then motor off astern. As outlined in Part One, displacement boats are often difficult to handle slowly astern, whilst small planing boats are likely to be swamped when manoeuvring astern off a lee shore.

Before making the approach to pass the heaving line, ensure that the dinghy crew is ready for action. Once you are in position with your heaving line thrown to the dinghy crew, your own manoeuvrability will be limited and so you want to be in that position for as short a time as possible.

Further action

When the dinghy has been righted or recovered from a lee shore, a decision has to be taken about further action. If the crew are able to continue the activity, the safety boat can depart.

If the crew decide they want to return ashore, or if the safety boat skipper makes that decision for them, the simplest option might be to lower the mainsail and return ashore under jib alone. This is always preferable to towing if the crew are capable of getting ashore, for it frees the safety boat for other work.

If a tow is required, then appropriate action should be taken as detailed below. Throughout a tow, the safety boat crew must be prepared to divert to another incident.

Abandoning dinghies

There will be incidents where the only priority is to get the dinghy crew ashore as quickly as possible. A capsized monohull in deep water will not drift far; even if close to shore, any damage on stranding will be a minor consequence compared to safety of life.

A deliberately abandoned dinghy should have a buoy or fender tied at or near the masthead. Not only will this prevent an inversion, but it indicates no others that a rescue has been made.

The larger the area of water, the more important is this warning, because of the time you are likely to be away from the dinghy. If conditions allow, it is even better to anchor the dinghy so that its position will be known when time allows recovery.

In coastal waters, it may be prudent to advise HM Coastguard by VHF of your action, to avoid false alarms.

If the dinghy is holed or the buoyancy is ineffective and it cannot be taken in tow, at least attach a long line securely to it and buoy the other end with a fender. You will then be able to locate it later when an attempt can be made to recover it.

SUMMARY OF KEY POINTS
★ Help the dinghy crew to help themselves before taking over.
★ Prompt action "walking the mast up" may be all that is required.
★ Once you take over, get the crew into the safety boat before dealing with the capsize.
★ When involved with one boat, keep a lookout for other incidents which may take priority.
★ There's no special mystique to singlehanders or multihulls.

Communication

Communication usually starts before any physical contact is made between tug and tow and finishes only when the tow has been completed.

The comments made in Part One all apply:

★ Never try to shout instructions from a moving powerboat

★ If you need to warn the dinghy crew of your intentions, take up position within earshot and shift into neutral so that you can be heard without shouting

★ Use as few words as possible

★ Ensure that your instructions have been heard by asking for an acknowledgement

★ Agree a simple set of arm signals for the tow. These could be based on those used for driving for turns and slowing down, and should include one for casting off the tow (a finger drawn across the throat is usually understood).

Towing Alongside

Most frequently seen as a salvage operation of a waterlogged dinghy, this method is convenient and quick. It is also the only way to manoeuvre a disabled vessel into a confined space, such as a pontoon berth.

Its main disadvantage are that it tends to be a rather wet tow except at low speed and requires good fendering between the boats.

For a straight tow, only the bow line and back spring (from bow of tug to quarter of tow) are needed, but for manoeuvring the head spring and stern line are necessary too.

The two key points for successful manoeuvring are:

★ The rudder (or outboard) of the tug must be astern of the tow

★ The tug's bow must be "toed-in" to the tow.

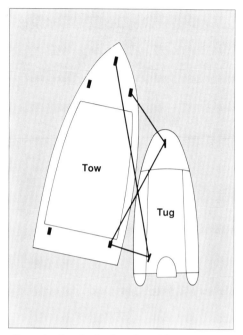

Correct set-up for towing alongside

Get these right and the tow will handle as one boat. Forget them and manoeuvring will become difficult or even impossible.

Passing the Tow Line

If the sails have not yet been lowered, the dinghy crew should be instructed to heave to and await instructions.

In flat water the safety boat will simply lie alongside, usually to windward, and the necessary securing can be done quite easily.

Note that the approach to a sailing dinghy may differ from advice given about approach to other craft. This is because of the obstruction caused by the boom and sail(s) to leeward.

In rough weather the safety boat should stand off to windward. If conditions are such that a heaving line cannot be thrown, a buoyed line can usually be floated downwind with a fender as the buoy.

Securing the Tow Line

Having made the transfer, the tow line has to be secured to the tow in such a way as to transmit the strain over the whole boat and not just to one cleat or post unless the post is designed for this purpose.

The stemhead fitting should not be used. The best option is to secure the tow by taking two turns around the mast (unless it is deck-stepped) or around the midships thwart. The end of the line can then be held by the dinghy crew without difficulty, with the advantage that it can be released quickly.

The line should be led through a fairlead at the dinghy's bow. If one isn't fitted, the painter or another line can be used to keep the towline close to the forestay. The strain of the towline should not be taken on the forestay itself.

Displacement safety boats are likely to have substantial cleats or posts at each quarter. Outboard powered safety boats should be fitted with a rope bridle running from the strongeyes or cleats on either side of the stern. The towline can then be secured to this bridle to avoid fouling the engine when manoeuvring.

The knot securing the towline should be capable of quick release. Chafe at this point is reduced if a round turn and bowline is used, rather than simply a bowline. Another option is to make one end of the bridle capable of quick release.

If the towline has to be made up of two or more lengths of line knotted together, the double sheet bend has the advantages of security and being easily undone.

Taking the Strain and Towing

A critical point occurs when the strain is taken on the towline, so the tug should start off slowly. Beware also of feet or hands being caught in a bight in the line as the strain is taken.

The length of the line should be such that the tug and tow are effectively one wavelength apart; i.e. in successive troughs and crests at the same time. The exception to this will be if you have to tow a waterlogged dinghy astern, when the towline should be adjusted so that the tow

rides with its bow up on the stern wave of the tug, rather than with a bows-down attitude on the face of the stern wave.

The longer the line, the greater the scope for smooth manoeuvring in open water, but the greater the difficulty when manoeuvring in confined areas. All turns should be made as wide as possible, and only after indicating to the tow.

If the towline is continually being jerked in heavy seas, a weight (perhaps a small anchor) can be slid down the tow rope to act as an "angel" or spring.

The greatest difficulty with towing light dinghies occurs when travelling downwind, when the dinghy may start to surf and overtake or even collide with the tug.

Reduce the risk of collision by lengthening the line, or avoid surfing by using a bucket as a drogue.

Being Towed

The instructions to those being towed in a dinghy are simple:
- ★ lower and stow the mainsail
- ★ raise the centreboard
- ★ sit well aft
- ★ steer to follow the safety boat.

Those sailing singlehanders may have difficulty lowering the sail, so the options are to unfasten the clew and if possible roll the sail around the mast or, in the case of the Optimist, simply remove the sprit.

Daggerboard dinghies can become very wet under tow, due to the water forced up and out of the case if the daggerboard is removed completely. The helmsman could therefore be advised either to raise the daggerboard as far as possible but leave it in its case or to lay the board over the top of the case to reduce splashing.

Towing a Disabled Dinghy

The only disabilities likely to affect the way a dinghy is towed are if it is badly holed, if the buoyancy has been compromised, if the rudder is broken/lost or if the crew is not aboard.

If holed, the dinghy should be heeled to keep the hole above the waterline and the displacement reduced if possible by removing the crew. This implies an alongside tow. Similarly, if the boat is waterlogged, tow it alongside.

Three of the problems listed above can be handled by towing the dinghy stern-first. This method is particularly effective when towing an unmanned dinghy, which otherwise shows an alarming tendency to yaw. By towing stern-first, the deep, sharp forefoot of many dinghies acts as a skeg to aid directional stability.

Exactly the same principle applies when dealing with a broken or lost rudder, or a dinghy whose bow buoyancy has been lost.

The towline should be secured to a bridle made up across the dinghy's stern, which in turn should spread the load to strong points, or around the whole hull.

Multiple Towing

When two dinghies have to be towed, the procedure could follow those outlined above for alongside or astern tows. The only additional precaution is that, if the dinghies are towed from each quarter of the tug, they should be fendered on the sides which could meet each other.

When more than two dinghies have to be towed, two entirely different methods can be used.

The first is simply to tow them in line, with each boat's painter made fast to the dinghy in front. The limitation on this is that the dinghy nearest the tug is taking the strain of all the others on its gear.

Teaching establishments which habitually use this technique to tow their fleets out to operating areas remote from their launching site modify the gear accordingly, with oversize painters and bow fenders to reduce damage in shunting. The last helmsman in line tends to steer the whole tow and must be properly briefed.

The alternative is the "herringbone" tow, where the tug is equipped with a very long towline, preferably fitted either with loops or with strops at intervals. This line is streamed astern of the tug so that dinghies can be attached as necessary, tying their painters to the loops or strops.

It is important for manoeuvrability that individual painters should not be led from the bow, but from much closer to the pivot point of each dinghy (normally near the mast). Centreboards should be partially lowered and each dinghy should be steered on a parallel course to the tug.

The herringbone tow can also be adopted using a long towline without special loops or strops, with each dinghy crew attaching their painter with a rolling hitch. This technique should only be used with experienced dinghy sailors, who can estimate the right distance between successive boats and who can be relied upon to tie an effective hitch. If tried with beginners, the result is a logjam of boats at the end of the towline!

Under no circumstances should boats being towed be allowed to tie the main towline round any part of their boat. To do so would make it impossible for them to cast off quickly and smoothly as required.

Casting Off the Tow

When casting off a multiple or single tow at sea, the tug should round up into wind so that sails can be raised before the dinghies cast off in order.

When towing a boat or fleet towards the shore, it is often possible for the tug to take the tow right to the beach, slipway or jetty, or for the dinghies simply to cast off near the shore, and paddle or drift in.

Delays in casting off are inevitable when towing beginners, so a more controlled alternative is for the safety boat to anchor so that each dinghy crew can sort themselves out then detach at leisure and paddle, row, drift or sail to the shore.

SUMMARY OF KEY POINTS

★ Successful towing alongside depends on the tug's positioning.
★ Agree arm signals before starting a tow.
★ Use a bridle to keep the towline clear of the tug's engine.
★ Spread the load of the towline on dinghy strongpoints.
★ One end of the towline must be capable of quick release.
★ Consider a stern-first tow if the dinghy is disabled.

Windsurfing has been part of the sailing world for at least 15 years. Since boards first appeared, concern has been expressed - both by those faced with rescuing them and by windsurfers themselves - about the techniques needed. With greater integration of the sport this concern will eventually disappear and to this end Windsurfer Rescue is part of every RYA Safety Boat course.

As the word "windsurfer" can be applied both to the equipment and the user and could cause ambiguity, in this chapter the person sailing a windsurfer is referred to as the sailor.

The recovery of any craft has its dangers. By the nature of the mobility of the rig, a windsurfer in a strong wind has particular risks. It is clearly preferable for safety boats operating in locations regularly frequented by windsurfers to be manned by trained personnel who are themselves active in the sport.

The popular types of planing craft detailed in Part One are ideal for windsurfer rescue. Larger displacement boats, with high freeboard and rig-destroying fittings are totally unsuitable.

Windsurfer rescue has a number of specific problems:

★   A windsurfer which has effectively capsized, with the sailor in the water, is very difficult to see in choppy conditions from water level. A special watch may need to be kept.

★   Windsurfers practising or waiting to waterstart may be quite happy one moment, then very cold and tired the next.

★   There are two main types of windsurfer sail. The beginners' type is comparatively simple to derig, but the fully-battened rig used on high performance boards needs care and understanding to dismantle without damage. A safety boat crew unfamiliar with the equipment should leave the sailor to dismantle his own gear.

It is recommended that anyone undertaking more than the very occasional club safety boat duty should learn the techniques of derigging boards and practise ashore whenever possible.

Approach

When a windsurfer has been capsized for more than about 30 seconds, the rig will act as a drogue or sea anchor and the board will drift downwind, leaving the mast pointing approximately head to wind.

Approach in light winds (A)

(A) In light winds, the quickest approach is to arrive at the masthead with the safety boat heading in the same direction as the board. The rig can then be pulled across the safety boat and the sailor brought aboard.

Approach in strong winds or with novices (B)

(B) In strong winds or with an inexperienced sailor, the approach should be made from downwind or, with care, across the wind. Once again, both bows should be in the same direction.

In all cases, the safety boat engine should be cut in the final approach until sailor and rig are aboard.

The approach to a windsurfer stranded on a lee shore will depend on weather conditions and the location. In light winds and flat water the safety boat might be able to get in close enough for a direct recovery without beaching.

The alternatives are to land, sort out the windsurfer and tow it off again (see below) or to ask the sailor to paddle the board clear of the shore and proceed as in (A) above.

In stronger winds, lee shore operations should follow the pattern outlined on page 22, with the sailor being asked to derig his board before being towed off to the anchored safety boat.

Recovery of Personnel

Once the safety boat is alongside, it will be easier for the sailor to get aboard the boat directly from the board after raising the daggerboard.

The safety boat coxswain holds the windsurfer steady while the sailor gets aboard the boat

If the sailor is feeling cold, he should sit low down in the boat to reduce further heat loss while the crew deal with the board. If the sailor is injured, unconscious or suffering from hypothermia, following immediate first aid he should be taken ashore and the board left to be recovered

by others or abandoned temporarily. Ideally, it will be marked to show that a rescue has taken place, possibly with a fender attached by a short line.

Recovery of Single Board Without Derigging

When using approach (A), the head of the sail should be brought across the safety boat until the board is close alongside. The sailor then comes aboard the safety boat and sits holding the mast firmly with the boom either inside or outside the boat.

The sailor holds the mast firmly with the boom either inside or outside the boat

In smaller safety boats, the sailor can sit in the bow using the same method. This keeps the rig clear of the safety boat coxswain.

Recovery in a smaller boat, like a Commando, is easier if the sailor sits in the bow

Fast progress can now be made, assuming the daggerboard has been raised. This is the most common technique when all that is needed is a short tow to safety.

Windsurfer recoveries tend to be almost exclusively upwind but care should be taken when manoeuvring across or downwind as the rig could flip over.

When using approach (B), the sailor can easily be taken aboard but manoeuvring the rig from its upwind position across the boat can be cumbersome.

In larger boats, like this RIB, take the board into the boat for maximum speed and manoeuvrability

Manoeuvring the rig across the boat after approach B can be cumbersome

Two other techniques are available without derigging. The first is that after the sailor is aboard and the rig is across the boat, the board can be detached from the rig and towed astern.

Unfortunately, the towing eyes fitted to the majority of windsurfers are too small to accept anything but a thin line. All teaching establishment boards should be modified by attaching a permanent short loop of line to the towing eye to facilitate rescue. This will allow use of the towlines carried as part of the normal safety boat equipment.

Windsurfing clubs and sailing clubs with windsurfer fleets are encouraged to incorporate this modification into their requirements for boards.

The second, only possible with larger safety boats, achieves the maximum mobility for the boat. Here the board is detached from the rig but the board itself is brought right aboard the safety boat.

Regardless of which of these methods is used, great care must be taken when underway to ensure that the outhaul line at the end of the boom does not foul the propeller.

Stowing the Rig

Recovering a windsurfer without derigging is practical in the majority of locations for relatively short distances. In coastal swell, over a longer distance, or when attempting a multiple tow, it is far safer to derig.

To derig a beginners' sail (less than three battens) the rig should be detached from the board and held by the sailor while the board is attached to a towline or brought aboard.

Once the battens have been removed, the outhaul line can be released or cut and the boom swung up to the mast. The sail can then be rolled towards the mast and secured with the outhaul and/or the uphaul lines.

Fully battened sails will normally require complete derigging. Release the downhaul at the sail tack, detension all the battens (usually secured with simple straps and buckles) and remove the boom. Many modern booms have a clamp inhaul end which makes removal quite simple. Older types have a lashing secured by a cleat or knot.

The sail can then be removed from the mast completely, rolled from the head or tack in line with the battens and stowed with the rest of the rig.

When towing a board, use a long enough towline to avoid the problem of the board surfing on the boat's sternwave and catching up or event trying to overtake.

Towing Several Boards

Recovery of more than one board involves derigging all the sails and towing the boards astern. Competent sailors can be asked to derig their boards while the safety boat deals with others, returning to collect them when the operation is complete. Novices will need help in derigging.

With the sailors and rigs aboard the safety boat, the boards can be towed line astern on a single line, which is tied to each towing eye loop. In congested waters a more compact tow can be made if two lines of boards are towed, one from each quarter of the safety boat.

Stowing a fully-battened rig

Towing astern; the sailor can keep watch on the board, which is far enough astern to avoid surfing

SUMMARY OF KEY POINTS

★ All windsurfers should prepare for the possibility of towing by fitting a short permanent loop to their board towing eye.

★ Safety boats for windsurfing should be fast, have low freeboard and be capable of beaching.

★ In all recoveries, the sequence is the same: get the sailor aboard, deal with the rig, then deal with the board.

If providing safety cover for canoes or kayaks as part of a training course you will normally be there as a back up for the instructor. Normally the instructor is expected to undertake rescue and return students to their craft and the safety boat coxswain should always check whether his or her services are required, except in an obvious emergency. A system of communication between the coxswain and the canoeing instructor should be established at the outset.

The main thing to remember when rescuing a swamped kayak is that if one end of the boat is pulled of the water and emptied, leaving the other end flooded, the kayak is likely to break in half if the rescuer then levers down in order to raise and empty the flooded end. It is essential to achieve a gradual emptying by keeping the kayak horizontal on its side and exerting a steady pull on the cockpit rim until most of the water has been evacuated. It can then be lifted upside down onto the gunwhale of the safety boat and see-sawed until empty.

Canoes (open canoes) should be turned upside down and merely lifted from the water by one end and pulled across the safety craft.

The RYA booklet VHF Radiotelephony for Yachtsmen provides detailed information on the use of VHF equipment in the maritime environment, which, hitherto, has been the cheapest and simplest equipment for small craft use. This booklet would not, however, be complete without some general explanation of both the International Maritime Mobile Band and of the Citizens' Band.

VHF International Maritime Mobile Band

Each of the channels in the 156-174 MHz band is allocated to one of six specific purposes - distress, safety and calling: inter-ship: public correspondence: port operation: ship movement: and (in the UK only) yacht safety.

Channels M or M2 (157.85 and 161.425 MHz) may be used by marinas and yacht clubs which have their own base station for communications between a vessel and the yacht club headquarters.

They may be used to control safety boats or maintain contact between boats or a committee boat and the shore but may not be used for public correspondence.

Channel M2 has been introduced recently and only new sets have it fitted.

Channel 16 (156.80 MHz) is the VHF International Distress Safety and Calling Channel. All ships fitted solely with VHF radio telephones are required to maintain continuous watch on Channel 16 when at sea and the regulations state that they must be equipped to transmit and receive on this channel.

Channel 6 (156.300 MHz) is the primary inter-ship frequency and the regulations state that all ships equipped with VHF radio telephones must be able to send and receive on this channel.

Other inter-ship channels frequently in use are channels 8, 72 and 77 which are exclusively for inter-ship use and should be used in preference to others.

Channel 67 (156.375 MHz) is one of many inter-ship channels. It is used in the United Kingdom only for communication between small craft and HM Coastguard for the exchange of safety information in situations which do not justify the use of distress or urgency procedures.

Club or School Safety Operations

Clubs or teaching establishments may have a base station and communicate with safety boats on channel M or M2, having obtained a private mobile radio licence.

The issuing authority is the Radiocommunications Agency,
Wray Castle,
PO Box 5, Ambleside LA22 OBF
Tel: 01539 434662

Power Output and Supplies

Most small craft VHF radio telephones have power outputs which can be switched to either one watt or 25 watts. The lower power output should be used whenever possible (with a range of up to about three miles) since this limits interference with other users.

Hand-held sets usually have outputs of one watt or about five watts. Again, low power should be used when possible but this gives a very restricted range, owing to the (usually) low aerial position.

Some hand-held sets can be fitted with remote earphones and microphones, to overcome the difficulty of hearing and transmitting over engine noise.

Operating Rules

The extensive operating rules can be summarised for safety use as follows:

★ ALWAYS LISTEN BEFORE YOU CALL.
★ You must not transmit false or deceptive distress, safety or identification signals or transmit without identification and you must use the vessel's name or call sign
★ You must not make unnecessary transmissions nor transmissions of a profane, indecent or obscene nature. You may not use channels

other than those covered by the issued licence.
★ You must not divulge the contents or even the existence of correspondence transmitted, received or intercepted.
★ Before transmitting, try to ensure that your transmission will not interfere with any other communication already in progress. Wait for a break before transmitting.

Voice Technique

The need for clear speech on a radio telephone should be obvious. Keep the microphone a short distance in front of the mouth and speak clearly and slowly at a normal conversation level. The most common faults are to speak too close to the microphone and to speak too quickly.

You should also, when necessary, use the standard phonetic international alphabet and numberals to avoid ambiguity.

Sending Messages

Assuming that you are operating on Channel M and your base station has chosen to call itself "Beachbase" and your safety craft is called "Safety One" you should initiate a call as follows:

"Beachbase, this is Safety One, Safety One. OVER".

When Beachbase acknowledges your call, it can simply be "Safety One, this is Beachbase OVER". None of this "I am receiving you loud and clear" stuff which simply clutters up the air with useless chat. You then pass your message and complete it with the word "over", the invitation to reply.

A transmission is concluded with the word "out". Note that the phrase "over and out" so beloved of film script writers is a self-contradiction which highlights the incompetence of the speaker.

Distress Messages

The distress signal "Mayday" indicates that a vessel, aircraft or person is threatenend by serious and imminent danger and requires immediate assistance.

Where this is not fully justified the Urgency signal "Pan-Pan" may be used. This implies that there is a very urgent message to transmit concerning the safety of a vessel, aircraft or person.

It is possible that in a coastal area a safety boat might want to notify its base station of problems and request "internal" assistance. Such calls should be treated as part of normal traffic and be made on the normal working frequency. If operating in a crowded location, it is worth emphasising that outside assistance is not required.

Alternatively, if outside assistance is required, it can be requested on Channel 16 by a "Pan-Pan" or "Mayday" call and message. This should never be done unless the circumstances warrant the action which will follow such a call.

An example could be: "Pan-Pan, Pan-Pan, Pan-Pan - Hallo all stations - Hallo all stations - THIS IS - Safety One, Safety One, Safety One - Safety cover for racing fleet operating in area of Blankville Fairway Buoy inadequate - Request assistance - OVER".

Quite probably this will invoke a reply from HM Coastguard who will invite you immediately to switch to a working frequency (probably Channel 67). They will then co-ordinate rescue organisations. It is possible that they will choose a frequency to speak to lifeboats and helicopters and you find yourself excluded from your own safety operation. Don't worry; do what you can to "tidy up" everything in sight and stand by to render any assistance.

Citizens' Band

Since CB was legalised in the UK, it has been used by some inland sailing clubs and schools as a cheaper alternative to marine-band VHF. Licences are issued from Post Offices to use CB equipment.

The 27 MHz FM service provides 40 channels between 27.6 and 28 MHz with a transmitter power of four watts. The maximum range is about 10 miles.

The Home Office, in consultation with other bodies, has published a short code of practice which does not vary much from the procedure for operating marine VHF equipment.

Leave Channel 9 clear for emergencies. Whilst there is no official monitoring of this channel it is a useful method of obtaining voluntary assistance. If there is no answer on Channel 9 you may call for help on either Channel 14 or 19.

Channel 14 is the general calling channel. When you have established a contact you should move to another channel to hold your conversation.

Channel 19 is for "main road" users and is the one most frequently used by long-distance transport drivers.

To avoid interference problems, position your antenna as far away as possible from others and remember that you are not allowed to use power amplifiers.

Always listen before your transmit (with the "squelch" control turned fully down and "tone squelch" turned off if you have selective call facilities) to ensure that you will not be transmitting on top of any existing conversation.

Keep transmissions short and leave a short pause before replying.

Plain language is just as effective as CB slang.

Be patient with newcomers and assist them.

The notes which follow should not be regarded as a shopping list of equipment, but rather as a catalogue from which each club or establishment will choose the equipment needed according to the area of operation and proximity to facilities ashore.

- ★ Bower anchor, chain and warp
- ★ Spare anchor(s), chain and warp
- ★ Fenders and warps
- ★ Auxiliary engine (small outboard)
- ★ Oars or paddles
- ★ Boarding ladder
- ★ Fire extinguisher(s)
- ★ Engine tool kit
- ★ Spare propeller (and appropriate tools)
- ★ Spare fuel and funnel
- ★ Compass and charts
- ★ Buckets, bailers
- ★ Bilge pump(s)
- ★ Hand pump
- ★ Bellows (inflatables and RIBs)

- ★ Towline(s) - preferably 2 x 20m with snap hooks
- ★ Heaving line
- ★ Buoys/fenders for dinghy recovery
- ★ First Aid Kit
- ★ Resuscitation Kit
- ★ Large "survival" or polythene bag
- ★ Blankets
- ★ Dry clothing
- ★ Hot drink in an insulated flask
- ★ Distress flares - daylight smoke and pinpoint red
- ★ VHF radio telephone
- ★ Axe or bolt croppers
- ★ Bosun's bag containing spare shackles, cordage etc
- ★ Knife
- ★ Binoculars

All equipment must be stowed or secured in place and the crew must know how to use each item. The bitter end of anchor warps must be secured, preferably with a knot or lashing which can be undone easily in the event of a fouled anchor.

Whilst it would be inappropriate to recommend specific brands of boats, engines or equipment, the following notes suggest a minimum specification for safety boats used to support small fleets at sailing clubs or teaching establishments.

The boat should have inherent buoyancy, built in, preferably including closed-cell foam.

It should have low enough freeboard to give access to the boat from the water.

It should be fendered to allow it to come alongside dinghies without damage and it should be manoeuvrable at low speeds in strong winds.

Engine Installation

Assuming the engine is an outboard, the engine size and shaft length should conform to the boat manufacturer's specification. The fuel tank and battery (if fitted) should be adequately secured.

The engine clamps should be tight and secured to prevent accidental loosening under way. If provision is made on the engine, it should be secured by bolts through the boat's transom.

The single-lever remote control should be equipped with a safety latch to prevent accidental engagement of gears from neutral, and it should be sited with adequate clearance from the steering wheel. An isolation switch and kill-cord should be fitted.

Equipment - Inland Use

The following should be regarded as a minimum, and compared with the comprehensive list on the previous page. All equipment should be stowed or secured in place.

★ Paddles or oars
★ Buckets
★ Bridle secured to strong towing eyes
★ Towline
★ Spare starting cord and minimal tool kit
★ Man-sized polythene bag
★ First Aid Kit containing large wound dressings and triangular bandages in a watertight container.

Additional Equipment - Coastal Use

★ Bower anchor sufficient for safety boat and any towed craft
★ Chain and warp as appropriate to area
★ VHF Radio
★ Distress flares - orange smoke and pinpoint red
★ Auxiliary outboard or spare propeller (and means to change it).

It is strongly recommended that anyone planning to act as a safety boat coxswain or crew should undertake basic first aid training.

The skills which are most likely to be needed are:

★ Resuscitation
★ Treatment of hypothermia
★ Control of bleeding.

In the majority of serious incidents, the role of the safety boat crew will be to keep the casualty alive and prevent his condition deteriorating whilst returning to shore at the most comfortable speed to medical assistance. This requires a crew of two in the safety boat.

Resuscitation

The top priority with any casualty is summed up as the ABC of First Aid - Airway, Breathing, Circulation.

The technique is taught on every first aid course and described well in the First Aid Manual (see page 48). The disadvantage of most first aid courses is that they assume an environment with plenty of space around the casualty. That is one reason why the courses run by the Royal Life Saving Society are so valuable; they assume that you are working in or near the water.

It is clearly preferable - and safer - to give resuscitation in the safety boat, but if there is difficulty in getting the casualty out of the water, don't waste time.

It is not quite possible to give supported resuscitation alongside a boat holding the casualty's head in the correct position. Put one hand against the boat and support the casualty's neck on your arm.

Treatment of Hypothermia

Next to the immediate need for artificial resuscitation comes the treatment of hypothermia, signs of which are likely to be present in anyone who has spent much time in the water.

Those signs are progressive:

★ Complaining of cold
★ Pale skin
★ Skin abnormally cold to touch
★ Uncontrollable shivering replaced by lack of muscle co-ordination
★ Slurred speech
★ Comprehension dulled
★ Irrational behaviour
★ Pulse and respiration slow
★ Unconsciousness.

If the casualty is still shivering and only looking cold, time is on your side but if he has stopped shivering, or his muscles are in spasm, or he is confused and lethargic with ice cold hands and feet, he must be taken ashore immediately, abandoning the dinghy or windsurfer if necessary.

On the way, reduce further heat loss by placing the casualty in the "man-sized" polythene bag you keep aboard for the purpose, or wrap him up in windproof clothing and keep him low in the boat. If the casualty is unconscious, place him in the recovery position if possible and check his respiration frequently.

Never give alcohol and do not encourage excercise in an effort to "warm-up". In mild cases, you may give the casualty a warm, not hot, drink.

Control of Bleeding

Exert direct pressure and try to draw the edges of the wound together with your fingers. If the injury is to a limb, raise it to reduce the flow of blood. Apply a sterile dressing as soon as possible. If the casualty is conscious, he can maintain the pressure. If you suspect internal bleeding loosen the casualty's clothing, keep him quiet, watch respiration and pulse and get him ashore as quickly as possible to seek medical assistance.

Shock

Shock may accompany any injury. The casualty will look pale and his breathing will be shallow. He needs warmth, reassurance and fresh air.

Burns

Severe rope burns are rare in dinghy sailing but the following rules may be useful:

★ Do not pull away stuck clothing
★ Cool the burn immediately in cold (preferably fresh) water for several minutes.

If you must cover a burn, use gauze or clean, non fluffy material and cover it lightly. Never apply lotions, antiseptics or greases to any burns where the skin has been damaged. Remove rings because of swelling.

Blows to the Head; Concussion

Anyone who has been hit on the head by a boom could suffer concussion. Treat the casualty for shock; look for open wounds, cover them using a triangular bandage to hold the dressings in place and get him to hospital.

FIRST AID CHECKLIST

As with the Equipment Checklist, the list which follows may be inappropriate to groups working on very restricted waters, where any casualty is within a few minutes of adequate First Aid facilities ashore. Everything carried in a safety boat's first aid kit boat must be immediate and essential equipment.

3 Triangular Bandages
2 Large wound dressings BPC No.15
3 Medium wound dressings BPC No.13
3 Conforming bandages - one each of 10 cms, 7.5 cms & 5 cms
1 Crepe bandage 7.5 cms
1 Roll 2.5 cms adhesive waterproof strapping
1 Large box assorted elastic adhesive dressings
1 Eye pad
10 Sachets antiseptic wipes (eg "Mediprep")
1 pkt Sterile Suture Strips (adhesive) eg Steristrips
2 pkts (x 5) single sterile gauze swabs 7.5 cms
10 Paraffin gauze burn dressings, individually wrapped 10 cms
1 pr Stainless steel scissors - blunt/sharp end
1 pr Spade end tweezers - good quality
10 Protected safety pins - 5 large, 5 medium

Resuscitation kit
Survival or polythene bag.

The notes which follow are reproduced from the RYA Dinghy Sailing Beginners Handbook G3 and are included here for the benefit of safety boat crews who are not dinghy sailors. They are intended to show the techniques taught to beginners on RYA dinghy courses.

The Golden Rule is "Stay with the Boat". The following method of righting will work in most conditions but, even if you cannot get sailing again, don't be tempted to swim for the shore. The boat's inherent buoyancy will keep you afloat and out of the water, and it's much easier for others to see a capsized dinghy than a head in the water.

Step 1. Both the crew swim to the stern and the helmsman checks that the rudder is secure and not floating off. The crew finds the end of the mainsheet and gives it to the helmsman who, using it as a lifeline, swims around the outside of the boat to the centreboard case.

Step 2. The crew checks that the centreboard is fully down and the helmsman holds onto it to prevent the boat inverting.

Step 3. The crew finds the top(weather) jib sheet and throws it over to the helmsman who confirms that he has it.

Step 4. The crew lies in the hull facing forwards and floats above the side-deck, being sure not to hang on (his extra weight won't help the helmsman and indeed might make it impossible for the helmsman to right the dinghy).

Step 5. The helmsman either lies back straight in the water with his feet on the boat's gunwhale and hauls on the jib sheet or climbs onto the centreboard, keeping his weight as close to the hull as possible to avoid breaking the board, and hauls on the jib sheet to right the dinghy with the crew member in it.

Step 6. With the jib backed the dinghy is hove-to and the crewman is then able to help the helmsman aboard. In fact, the helmsman may find that he may be able to get half-way into the boat as it comes upright.

Some dinghies have the buoyancy distributed in a way which makes them turn completely upside down almost immediately. To counteract this, you should never hang onto the inside of the dinghy as you capsize, but simply drop into the water.

If the dinghy does invert, the easiest way to get it back onto its side is for the crew to press down on one side of the stern while the helmsman uses his weight and leverage on the centreboard. Then proceed as above.

Righting Singlehanders

If you are learning in a singlehanded dinghy, you will probably be briefed about capsize before you go afloat for the first time. Once again, the Golden Rule is "stay with the boat".

If the dinghy capsizes to leeward, climb over the edge of the hull and stand on the daggerboard where it emerges from the hull.
Hold onto the gunwhale, lean back and slowly pull the boat upright.

In a windward capsize you might be thrown out before the boat stops. Hold onto the mainsheet if possible, swim to the boat and hang onto the daggerboard. Your weight on the daggerboard may be enough to lift the mast and sail clear of the water, when the wind will take over and flip the boat upright.

If not, climb onto the daggerboard and pull gently on the hull to lift the mast just clear of the water. Hold the boat balanced in that position and let the wind push the whole boat around until the sail is downwind, when you can continue as outlined above.

If the dinghy inverts, pull the daggerboard out as far as possible. You might be able to right it by standing on the windward gunwhale, holding on to the daggerboard and leaning back. Some singlehanders respond better if you kneel on the bow when they flip over onto their sides.

Step 1

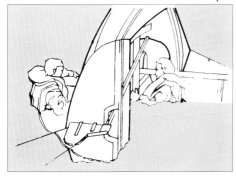

Step 2

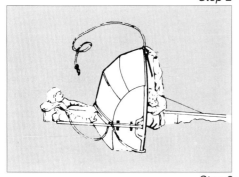

Step 3

Step 4

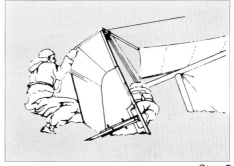

Step 5

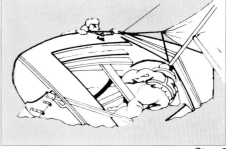

Step 6

Bailing

Modern dinghies will come upright with so little water aboard that you can sail on immediately, the self-bailers in the bottom of the hull being used as soon as you pick up speed.

Many older dinghies, however, will come up full of water, which must be bailed out. If the water level is above the top of the centreboard case, you will have to work fast or you will be fighting a losing battle. It should be clear that a bailer is an essential part of the dinghy's equipment. The worst bailer is one that floats away from the capsized boat, so make sure it is tied on.

BIBLIOGRAPHY

Around the Red Tape
ISBN 0 901501 31 X
                    Edmund Whelan
Royal Yachting Association
A handbook of law and administration for clubs and schools, written by the RYA Legal Manager

This is Boat Handling at Close Quarters
ISBN 0 7136 5840 1
Dick Everitt and Rodger Witt
                    Nautical Books
Well illustrated manual of handling techniques, particularly relevant to displacement boat manoeuvring.

Fast Boats and Rough Seas
ISBN 0 229 11840 2
                Dag Pike Adlard Coles
Advanced boat handling skills, written by a world leader.

RYA Booklets

In addition to Around the Red Tape mentioned above, the RYA publishes a wide range of booklets on different aspects of the sport. Those which are particularly relevant as background reading for safety organisers and crews include:
YR4   Club Race Officer's Handbook
G5   Weather Forecasts
G22   VHF Radio Telephony

Seamanship for Divers
ISBN 0 09 166291 5
                British Sub-Aqua Club
Comprehensive handbook covering everything from ropework and engine care to boat handling in inflatables and larger boats. Concise and well-illustrated.

First Aid Manual
ISBN 0 86318 230 5
                    Dorling Kindersley
The official manual of the three national organisations. Concisely written and very clearly illustrated. A recommended back-up to every first aid course and an essential book for every club and teaching establishment.

First Aid and Resuscitation
Dr. A. J. Handley   RLSS
Specifically written for lifeguards, this manual has a useful section on how to give resuscitation in the water.